meet the family
my Mum

by Mary Auld

W
FRANKLIN WATTS
LONDON · SYDNEY

This is Darren
and his mother.
Sometimes he calls
her 'Mummy' but
mostly just 'Mum'.

Sally grew inside
her mum's tummy
for nine months
before she was born.

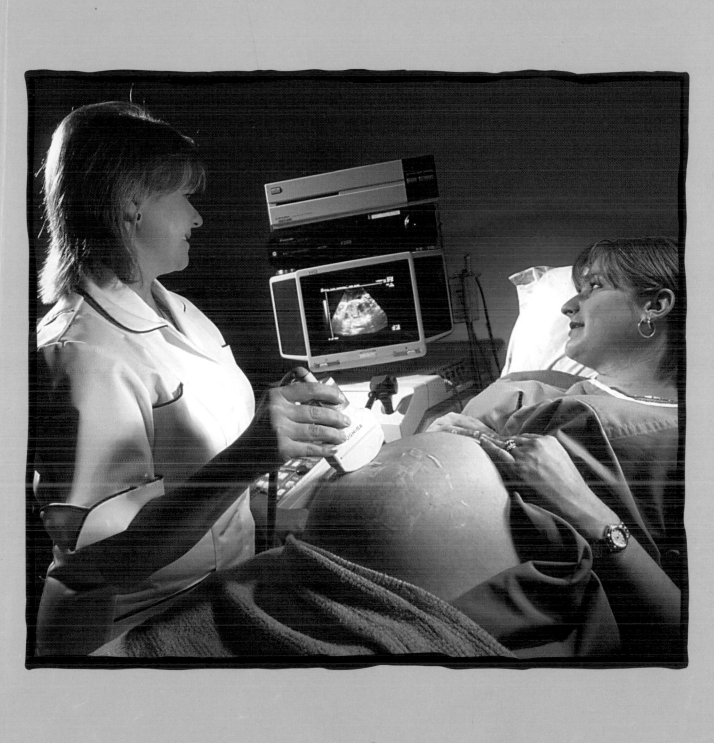

Jake was adopted when he was six weeks old. His mum has loved him ever since.

Lizzie has two mums.
Her step-mum lives with
her dad and Lizzie stays
with them at weekends.

David's mum
works in a hospital.

Chai's mum
works in an office.

Susan's mum is a teacher.

This is Maria
with her mum
and her mum's
mum – Maria's
granny!

What's your mum like?

Family words

Here are some words people use when talking about their mum or family.

Names for Mum:
Mother, Mummy, Mum, Ma, parent.

Names for Dad:
Father, Daddy, Dad, Pa, parent.

Names of other relatives:
Son, Daughter; Brother, Sister; Grandchildren; Grandparents; Grandmother, Granny, Grandma; Grandfather, Grandad, Grandpa; Uncle; Aunt, Auntie; Nephew, Niece.

If we put the word 'Step' in front of a relative's name, it means that we are related to them by marriage but not by birth.

When people are adopted, they become part of a family by law, although they were not born into that family.

A family tree

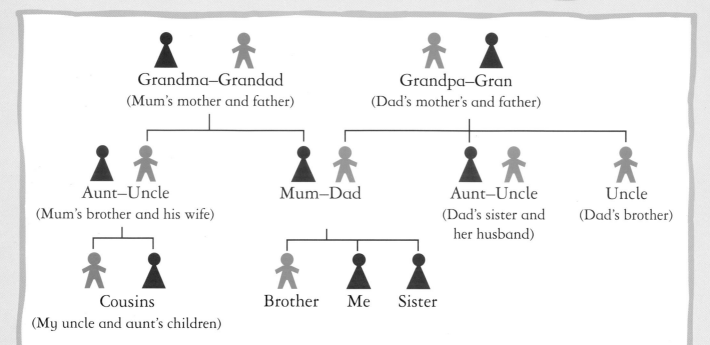

Grandma–Grandad
(Mum's mother and father)

Grandpa–Gran
(Dad's mother's and father)

Aunt–Uncle
(Mum's brother and his wife)

Mum–Dad

Aunt–Uncle
(Dad's sister and
her husband)

Uncle
(Dad's brother)

Cousins
(My uncle and aunt's children)

Brother   Me   Sister

You can show how you are related to all your family
on a plan like this one. It is called a family tree.
Every family tree is different. Try drawing your own.

First published in 2003 by Franklin Watts,
96 Leonard Street, London EC2A 4XD

Franklin Watts Australia
45-51 Huntley Street, Alexandria, NSW 2015

Copyright © Franklin Watts 2003

Series editor: Rachel Cooke
Art director: Jonathan Hair
Design: Andrew Crowson

A CIP catalogue record for this book
is available from the British Library.

ISBN 0 7496 4883 X

Printed in Hong Kong/China

Acknowledgements:
Peter Beck/Corbis: 11. Bruce Berman/Corbis:
front cover centre below. www.johnbirdsall.co.uk:
front cover centre top, 6, 7, 10, 12, 18. Deep
Light Productions/ Science Photo Library: 5.
Dex Images Inc/Corbis: 20-21. George
Disario/Corbis: 2. Carlos Goldin/Corbis: front
cover centre above. Don Mason/Corbis: 1, 13.
Brian Mitchell/Photofusion: 15, 19. Jose Luis

Pelaez/Corbis: front cover bottom. Ulrike
Press/Format: 17. George Shelley/Corbis:
front cover main, 22. Ariel Skelley/Corbis:
front cover centre, 8. Christa Stadtler/
Photofusion: 16.

Whilst every attempt has been made to clear
copyright should there be any inadvertent
omission please apply in the first instance to
the publisher regarding rectification.